Original title:
The Doorway to the Past

Copyright © 2025 Creative Arts Management OÜ
All rights reserved.

Author: Dorian Ashford
ISBN HARDBACK: 978-1-80587-123-1
ISBN PAPERBACK: 978-1-80587-593-2

Through the Veil of Memories

Once I tripped on my own shoe,
That was when I fell right through.
Lands of socks and mismatched shoes,
Dancing with my childhood blues.

Cartwheels made my tummy ache,
But who could doubt a ninja's fate?
Silly joys in every place,
Time to gallop in a race.

Windows to Forgotten Times

Peeking through a lacy drape,
I found my past in a funny shape.
A record player skipped and whirled,
While bubblegum threatened the world.

Old game consoles with dusty screens,
Passed down laughter, or so it seems.
Racing cars that bounce and fly,
In the realm where giggles lie.

Shadows of Yesterday's Embrace

In the attic, dust bunnies cheer,
A hide-and-seek party draws near.
The ghost of my cat plays a prank,
Hiding under an old paint bank.

Mismatched toys and smiles so bright,
Playing hide and seek at night.
The shadow laughed, oh what a sight,
Who knew nostalgia took flight?

Steps Back into Silence

Each creaky step tells a tale,
Of silly hats and a dancing snail.
A whisper from a box of toys,
Told secrets of our childhood joys.

I once scribbled on the wall,
With crayons, I was quite enthralled.
But now I'm just a little stuck,
In the echo of my own cluck.

The Timeworn Signpost

A signpost leaning, all askew,
Points to a time we never knew.
It says, 'Turn here, with a grin!'
'Watch for the laugh that roams within!'

With arrows twisting, paths unclear,
It beckons softly, 'Persevere!'
I giggle at the map's strange art,
The road of jest, a merry start!

Unveiling Hidden Pathways

Behind a bush, a door swings wide,
Inviting all to come inside.
A hallway filled with silly hats,
And rubber ducks that chatter chats!

Each step I take, I trip and laugh,
Stumbling through this funny graph.
With memories that dance and play,
I find the joy in yesterday!

Sliding Into the Calming Past

I found a slide with colors bright,
It took me back in sheer delight.
Down I go, with giggles loud,
Landing in a past, quite proud!

A bounce, a waddle, rounding bends,
Where socks and laughter never end.
Sliding back on whimsy's path,
I whirl through time, I do the math!

Shadows Caught in the Frame of Time

In frames of laughter, shadows dance,
Captured moments, a playful prance.
Each chuckle echoes through the air,
A snapshot taken, none can compare!

These figures twirl, in silly pose,
Like film actors in comical clothes.
They wave, they wink, and freeze with glee,
In this whimsical gallery of me!

Reflections on the Threshold

A squeaky hinge and a silly cat,
I slammed the door, now where's my hat?
Looking back at my old red chair,
It seems to laugh, but I don't care!

The ghosts of socks lay on the floor,
Did they just dance? I can't ignore!
I trip on memories, quite a sight,
Is that my lunch from last Tuesday night?

Steps Leading to Tomorrow's Ghost

I found a shoe that's clearly mine,
But it's missing its partner, oh how fine!
I step right over spaghetti stains,
Those were my friends, now stuck in chains.

Tomorrow knocks with a cheeky grin,
"Hey there, buddy, let's do this again!"
But I just wave and take a seat,
Enjoying snacks that can't be beat.

In the Company of Shadows

My shadows dance in a silly way,
They trip and tumble, brightening my day.
With hats and glasses, they play charades,
Do they know I'm the one who parades?

I giggle as they make silly faces,
In the old house filled with strange traces.
Each chuckle echoes off the walls,
Reminding me of the best of brawls.

Embracing Faded Footprints

Footprints in dust, oh what a mess,
Each step tells tales of my old dress.
Did I really dance on the kitchen floor?
It seems my slippers don't want to score!

With baby steps back to yesterday,
I find the old toys that love to play.
Catching laughs in the fading light,
I'm grateful for memories that feel just right.

Forgotten Footsteps

In a world where socks just disappear,
One mismatched pair, oh dear, oh dear!
They dance around, a lost ballet,
Whispers of days when kids would play.

Old shoes lean against the hall,
Telling tales of a time when they'd ball.
A squeaky toy from ages gone,
Now laughs in the sun like a joyful dawn.

A clock that ticks and tocks away,
Tickled by memories of yesterday.
Each sound it makes a giggle or two,
As if it knows our silly view.

The cat's old bed, a royal throne,
Where it ponders things long overgrown.
Did it chase mice in a life before?
Or just nap on cushions, a furry bore?

Echoing Hallways of History

In hallways wide where echoes play,
Ghosts of past pranks come out to sway.
A whoopee cushion from days gone by,
Still leaves the bravest quite shy.

There's a ladder once used for climbing high,
Now just leans like a sleepy guy.
Was it a hero or a drab old fool,
Who thought that trip to make him cool?

The portrait hangs with a crooked smile,
Wondering if it's been there a while.
With grandpa's hairdo, a sight to see,
He knew what cool really meant, teehee!

Footsteps dance like folks at a fair,
Socks and sandals, quite the pair!
In every creak, a story sings,
Of socks with stripes worn by kings!

A Glimpse Beyond the Frame

Through a dusty glass, I peer inside,
At photos grand where laughter died.
There's Uncle Joe with a pie on his face,
Forever caught in a clumsy grace.

A wedding gown from years of yore,
That once spun tales on the dance floor.
Its faded lace, now yellowed and torn,
Holds secrets of nights when we would scorn.

A rocking chair that squeaks just right,
It mocks the family's failed kite flight.
Each sway tells stories; a riddle anew,
Of windblown dreams that somehow flew.

In frames that warp and memories dense,
Lies laughter buried in each suspense.
With every glance, a giggle it brings,
As nostalgia dances and gently sings.

Fragments of Lost Moments

In a box of trinkets, memories sleep,
Old rubber bands and a tooth that'd leap.
Snapshots stick like gum on a shoe,
Tales of a time that once was true.

An empty candy wrapper, crinkled and torn,
Holds the essence of a kid reborn.
Silly notes written, oh what a fuss,
"I love you in math, but not on the bus."

A wristwatch cracked, but it still ticks on,
Remindful of hours that we've not drawn.
Time may slip, but we'll always keep,
The laughter sewn in moments deep.

A postcard penned to Aunt Sally's cat,
"Wish you were here!" oh imagine that.
Each fragment speaks with a wink and a cheer,
As we laugh at the past, year after year.

Gates of Remembrance

I found a key, it's shaped like cheese,
A door appeared with a gentle breeze.
I peeked inside, oh what a mess,
Old socks and snacks in a time-warp dress.

A turtle sang a tune out loud,
While a cat nap danced on a fluffy cloud.
The clock is ticking backwards with a frown,
As I chase my youth in silly clown town.

Each photo giggles, whispers my name,
I swear that jacket was once quite the fame.
But rust and dust are friends I see,
No one told me age is comedy.

With laughter ringing through golden halls,
I trip on memories, oh how it enthralls!
Through laughter and echoes, we wander and play,
In this wacky world of yesterday's fray.

The Echoes We Carry

I hear my past calling, with a honk and a beep,
It says, 'Remember that time you fell fast asleep?'
Behind the curtain, a squirrel gives chase,
Chasing the echoes of my younger face.

Old bicycles squeak and wobbly knees,
Remind me of summers and sticky ice cream freeze.
The laughter of friends wrapped in bright hues,
Pillow fights turning into playful ruse.

Ghosts of my choices tap dance around,
Bringing the memories that once had me bound.
We chuckle at blunders, some wise, some absurd,
The best kind of tales are wild and deferred.

A toad in a hat croaks, "Time's just a jest,"
We clutch at the past but it's all just a fest.
Each giggle and gaffe, another sweet prize,
In the world of our stories, the past never lies.

Veils of Yesterday's Light

In a box of shadows, I found my old shoes,
With laces that giggle and blisters to lose.
Each step I take feels like dance with the past,
Stumbling through rabbit holes, oh what a blast!

A sneeze sets off a parade of old friends,
Barreling in laughter that never quite ends.
"Who let the spiders out?" someone will shout,
As we tap our toes to the memories about.

The candy I hoarded, a treasure I kept,
Counts as a crown where my giggles adept.
Riding on memories like waves in the night,
Veils lift away, revealing pure delight.

So here we are, in a carnival spin,
Chasing lost moments that rattle within.
With slingshots of joy flinging us back,
In this land of memories, nothing we lack.

Ghosts in the Halls of Memory

In halls filled with whispers, I meet a lost sock,
Its words are like magic, they tick-tock and knock.
It tells tales of bouncing, of laundry gone wild,
With giggles and grumbles of a once-happy child.

A ghost with a bow tie polishes dreams,
While juggling old stories and silly ice creams.
He winks with a grin and hiccups a cheer,
Let's toast to the cringes we hold so dear.

Through closets of chaos and keepsakes galore,
Each item a chuckle, a glimpse at the score.
Strange hats and odd toys all come out to play,
As ghosts in the halls remind us to sway.

With mischief afoot, my past joins the fun,
An orchestra's playing, we're all on the run.
In shadows of laughter, we hold hands so tight,
As ghosts of our journeys dance bold in the light.

The Mosaic of Memories

In a corner hangs a photo frame,
Of Uncle Joe, still playing the game.
His pants are up, his tie's a mess,
We laugh and cringe, we must confess.

A birthday cake that tips and sways,
Oh how we loved those sugar days!
Each bite a giggle, each crumb a tale,
Of frosting fights that never fail.

A sock lost long in wash's churn,
Returns to tell where it did burn.
With each new scratch, our tales unfold,
We gather 'round, both young and old.

So here we sit, with tea in hand,
Recalling quirks that life had planned.
In laughter's tune, we find our trace,
In this collected, silly space.

Steps into the Heart of Time

Each step we take, a creak or squeak,
In shoes too tight or overly chic.
The dance of dots upon the floor,
Each one a story, each one a roar.

Old books with spins and paperbacks,
Reveal the facts and all the hacks.
Dare we read about the past?
For surely, time cannot go fast!

A glance at Grandma's awkward dress,
Where fashion plates can't quite impress.
We laugh at styles we thought were bold,
Wondering how they ever sold!

So come along and take a peek,
At memory lane's charming freak.
With each turn, come joyful cries,
In steps of fun, our hearts will rise.

Hidden Time Capsules

In dusty rafters, treasures hide,
A tin of cookies, stale inside.
We munch on crumbs, the joke's on us,
As flavors fade, so does the fuss.

Old comic books from days of yore,
With caped crusaders and bright galore.
We flip through pages, quirks on show,
With cheesy plots we used to know.

A diary with secrets sillier still,
Each page reveals our childhood thrill.
With doodles funny, and notes of glee,
We snicker hard at our old decree.

So dig it out, dust off the lid,
Recall those days, never quite hid.
Laughter echoes, memories swell,
In hidden gems, we weave our spell.

Doorways of Distant Dreams

Through the archway, into delight,
A world of whimsy, bursting bright.
With dreams that dance and play so free,
We strut our stuff in jubilee.

A hat too big or shoes too wide,
The laughter spills, we cannot hide.
Each corner turned, another jest,
In this wild space, we feel the best.

A time machine with squeaky wheels,
Takes us back to childhood meals.
We slurp and spill in messy pride,
With memories close, nowhere to hide.

So join the fun, let echoes chime,
In distant dreams, we twist our rhyme.
With giggles shared and tales retold,
We dance through life, both brave and bold.

Sagas of Silence

In a room packed tight with dust,
Old photographs are all we trust.
Great Uncle Joe with socks so bright,
He fought the laundry, won the fight.

My grandma's tales of love and woe,
With mismatched socks, she stole the show.
Her secrets hid in cookie jars,
While grandpa danced like he was Mars.

A letter found, the ink is blurred,
It tells of dreams that went unheard.
Yet laughter echoes through the years,
As we still toast to all our fears.

So raise your glass, let's have some fun,
With tales of old, we'll never run.
In silent rooms where whispers creep,
The funny memories we still keep.

Windows into Yesteryear

Through windows cracked, the sun leaks in,
And tells us stories where we've been.
My sister's hair, once bright and green,
Bewildered me when I was a teen.

My dad's old chair, it creaks and sighs,
While grandma's tales just morph and rise.
With every word, a giggle bursts,
At awkward lunches, that's just the worst.

The cat that pranced on grandma's lap,
Dressed like a royal, made me clap.
And uncles who would take the bait,
Of silly pranks that tempt their fate.

We see the past through glasses thick,
And joke about our cousin's trick.
With every glance, we find a card,
In windows wide, we play our bard.

Thresholds of Yesteryear

At the threshold, shoes untied,
In my youth, I would collide.
With bikes and dreams of summer sun,
We raced the wind, oh what a run.

The laughter echoing through the halls,
Where each funny prank still enthralls.
A stash of toys from years gone by,
Each box a time capsule, oh my!

Granddad's pipe, his favorite chair,
Held scents and stories, a little flair.
My aunt who danced like no one watched,
With moves so wild, she nearly botched.

The silly games we played till night,
With shadows creeping, giving fright.
Yet on this brink of old and new,
We send up laughter, just us few.

Echoes Beneath the Arch

Beneath the arch, we found our laughs,
With silly pictures, we made gaffes.
A pie in Grandma's face was gold,
Her laughter rich, her fun untold.

The dog with socks, snug on his paws,
Would chase his tail without a cause.
And every echo sang of glee,
In moments shared, just you and me.

A ghost we made with bedsheet flair,
Naïve, we thought we had a scare.
Yet all we heard were fits of giggles,
As we both danced like two big wiggles.

So let us stroll and reminisce,
In every arch, find joy and bliss.
For hilarity's the best of friends,
In every heart, the laughter bends.

The Archway of Past Sorrows

In a hallway of socks, where lost things reside,
I found my old shoes, they don't fit quite right.
A photo of me, with hair made of cheese,
Wishing for glamour, but got giggles with ease.

Echoes of laughter from days long ago,
When dancing with brooms was the height of my glow.
My history's silly, a colorful mess,
But who wouldn't want a past full of jest?

A hat from a party where I wore it askew,
With glitter and nonsense, oh what a debut!
Time-traveling blunders, each step is a laugh,
In a world of my quirks, I'm my own epitaph.

Encrypted Memories

There's a box in the attic with secrets inside,
A chicken dance video, oh how I have tried.
To unlock the laughter, the joy it will reap,
  Yet every time I play it, I fall into sleep.

Maps drawn by crayons of places I've faked,
You'd think I was heading to a big pie bake.
With arrows to 'nowhere' and X's that tease,
My treasure's a giggle, oh that's quite a breeze!

In rows of old photos, my past haunts my day,
Wearing sunglasses at night, what was I to say?
A wizard's great cape, a sergeant's headband,
  Lost in these memories, I don't understand!

Mysterious Gateways of Time

There's a portal in my closet, or so I have dreamed,
Where mismatched socks chatter, their fortune they schemed.
I bet they tell tales of their great escapades,
But most are lost stories tucked under the shades.

Each flip on the calendar brings giggles and flair,
Like times when I tried wearing last season's hair.
The mirror reflects some bewildered old me,
What in the world could that hairstyle be?

These gateways to silliness twist and they swirl,
As I bonk my head lightly on fabric unfurl.
Laughter is key, even time's in disguise,
Each memory tickles, bringing fun to my eyes.

Silhouette of What Once Was

In the shadows of memories, they dance and they prance,
A sock puppet show, oh give them a chance!
A turtleneck sweater that's three sizes too small,
Yet somehow I wore it, I still stand tall.

Pictures from picnics, where ants stole the bread,
Enticing my friends with a grin and a spread.
We laughed till we cried, planning food fights with wit,
In the silhouettes of joy, we embraced every bit.

A glittery history like stars in the night,
With each goofy moment, I twinkle with delight.
So here's to the quirks that our past days extoll,
For the funny, the silly, make up my whole!

Ancestral Echoes

In the attic, dust bunnies play,
Old portraits laugh at us every day.
Great Uncle Larry wore a pink dress,
We're glad he enjoyed that funky mess!

A grandma's quilt tells silly tales,
Of family feasts and crazy gales.
When Aunt Judy danced with a broom in hand,
We still wonder if it was all just planned!

Cousins argue about who's the best,
Trainwreck karaoke? Who had the zest?
Uncle Joe thinks he can still out-sing,
But we all know he can't catch a thing!

Echoes of laughter fill every room,
As we dive deep into the family tomb.
Each tale we share brings a chuckle or two,
Ancestral echoes, always anew!

Breadcrumbs of Time

Follow the crumbs of yesterday's bread,
Through awkward dances and lines that we've said.
A recipe card with stains and a smudge,
What was that secret? We can only fudge!

Grandpa's fishing tales grow taller each year,
While Grandma's socks? They're never quite near.
We search for the hats that once ruled our heads,
Only to find them inside shoe sheds!

Time-traveling phone calls, we jest and we tease,
"Why'd you buy that suit?" "For a next-century breeze!"
The family tree looks more like a bush,
Stuck in the past, it gives us a rush!

Breadcrumbs of laughter paved paths through the night,
With ancestors smirking, hidden from sight.
Each moment we share, now it's carved in rhyme,
With love from the past, we're outliving time!

Veils between Now and Then

Lift the veil, peek behind the screen,
See wacky fashion, all in-between.
A tuxedo shirt with polka-dot pants,
Uncle Frank's style made everyone dance!

Old family videos, fuzzy and bright,
We can't stop laughing, it's a comical sight.
Auntie mimics the dog, oh what a show,
Her talent for howling, a family pro!

Photos reveal all our past escapades,
From pickle-eating contests to weird parades.
Great-Grandma's smirk is a real work of art,
As she holds up a fish—was it caught or was smart?

Veils between then and our whacky now,
Each moment unfolds, and we wonder how.
History's antics, all shined in light,
A comedy wrapped in our shared delight!

Scenes from a Worn Threshold

Steps creak loudly, a reliable sound,
As ancient jokes echo all around.
"Remember the time?" sparks laughter anew,
Grandpa's old sneakers? They flew like a shoe!

The worn threshold bears tales of its own,
Of cousins and cousins who've grown and have grown.
Silly arguments that made no sense,
Did we really claim that fence was immense?

Sipping sweet tea on a quirky old chair,
"Time travel's possible, if you just dare!"
The clock's hands spin in a nonsensical race,
With wild family antics we can't help but trace.

Scenes unfold like a scripted play,
With actors who laugh at the roles they portray.
Through the doorway of memories, we all converge,
In a whirl of joy, where past and now merge!

Bridges to Forgotten Histories

Old photos freeze a silly smile,
With disco shoes and lots of style.
Each laugh echoes in the air,
As we trip on our own affair.

Grandma danced on kitchen tiles,
With a broom and goofy styles.
She sang out loud, the cat would stare,
Wonders lost, but laughs in the air.

Digging through the attic's dust,
We find treasures, just for a rust.
A hat from prom, a broken toy,
Each relic sparks up ancient joy.

With every step on memory's bridge,
A silly tale makes the heart spin.
We'll giggle 'til the day ends bright,
Past and present dancing in light.

Footprints in the Sand of Time

Footprints trace where laughter leans,
On a beach of forgotten scenes.
We built a castle made of lies,
Where seagulls squawk and time flies.

Ice cream dribbles down our hands,
As we sketch out silly plans.
A wave crashes, taking our grin,
Leaving behind a waterkin.

Chasing crabs that scurry fast,
Making memories that will last.
"Hey, did you step on that shoe?"
"Take it back, it doesn't belong to you!"

In the sand, a treasure map,
Leading to giggles, maybe a nap.
As the tide rolls in with a roar,
We leave our footprints, wanting more.

Recalling the Unwritten Pages

Pages faded, whispers sweet,
Of adventures imagined on the street.
We scribbled dreams in crayon bright,
With unicorns taking flight.

A treehouse made of quirky plans,
Where we hosted parties for our fans.
"What's that smell? Oh, burnt popcorn!"
A masterpiece at every dawn.

Daydreams swirling like cotton fluff,
Where silly things are never enough.
A knight with armor made of foil,
Taking on monsters, fueling our toil.

With crayons tucked and pages turned,
We find humor in lessons learned.
Every line a joyful surprise,
In the book where laughter lies.

Portals to Echoed Joys

Open a door, hear the giggles,
Of folks in hats, doing the wiggles.
Silly moments capture our glee,
With friends who sing off-key, oh me!

A toast with soda, and pop rocks too,
We're time travelers, just me and you.
With wigs that bounce and shoes that squeak,
Every glance shares secrets, unique.

Jumping into the past's embrace,
Wearing mismatched socks for extra grace.
The clock spins, but don't you fret,
For laughter's the best we can get.

Through the echoes, we navigate,
Finding joy in all that we create.
As giggles swirl and memories spark,
In our hearts, joy leaves a mark.

Reflections in Dusty Glass

I stared at my reflection, quite a sight,
A wild hairdo that could cause some fright.
My grandma's old dress, too bright for my taste,
It looks like a rainbow threw up in haste.

In dusty glass I see past blurry cheer,
A time when my outfits drew laughter and fear.
My past closet's wonders, like monsters, they loom,
Who knew fashion could come from a haunted room?

Old photos reveal a dance of such grace,
My aunts took swings like they'd trip on their lace.
We giggled through parties and tea gone awry,
Now I just wonder how time flew so high.

I wipe the glass clear, a ghost of my style,
In cringey old outfits, I can only smile.
The jokes that we shared in our brightly-hued flair,
Are treasures that linger through dust and through air.

Chasing the Flicker of Old Flames

I stumbled on memories flickering bright,
Old flames that could roast marshmallows all night.
With hairdos of high and pants way too tight,
I wonder if dating was always this trite?

We danced at the prom, all wigs and big shoes,
I slipped on my date, left him singing the blues.
Our love notes were scribbled on napkins and tags,
Now they sit in a box marked "Things that are drags."

One guy thought he'd charm me with his magic tricks,
He vanished on stage, and it felt like pure mix,
With rabbit and hat, he just lost to the ground,
Perhaps my heart's still there, waiting to be found.

I laugh at the stories of love gone askew,
Chasing old flames that, well, never quite grew.
Yet in the ashes, there's warmth and delight,
It's fun to relive what was kismet that night.

Ancestral Footsteps

In shoes too big, I trudge through the past,
My great-great-granddad must've danced quite fast.
With every step, I hear echoes of cheer,
I hope they wore socks, or it's foul down here!

The family tree, a maze of odd branches,
Where everyone bickers and takes wild chances.
A grand-aunt who claimed she could speak to the skies,
Though all we got back was three angry flies.

They say my great-uncle invented the grill,
But all I found were burnt burgers and thrill.
His recipes mixed laughter with charcoal delight,
And everyone argued on what tasted right.

I trace the old paths as I cackle and grin,
With each twisted tale, I tuck my chin in.
Ancestral steps, with their whimsical flair,
Show how life's a dance, if you dare and you dare!

The Past Calls Softly

My phone buzzes lightly, it's calling my name,
A voice from the past, and it's sounding quite lame.
"Remember the time when you fell down the stairs?"
Thank you, dear cousin, for our shared little flares.

Soft whispers of yesteryears tickle my ear,
Like kittens on couches, both fuzzy and dear.
My childhood was filled with sweet laughter and dough,
With friends who had secrets that we'd never show.

But now as I listen, I think of the fun,
Of mischief and trouble under the sun.
The past laps at my feet like a dog on a spree,
Making me giggle, oh why can't it be?

I'll hold on to laughter, let it drift like a tune,
While memories waltz 'neath the light of the moon.
The past gently tugs at my heart with a jest,
A tickle of joy that simply won't rest.

When Windows Used to Open

Once I had a window wide,
But now it just won't slide.
I push and pull, it's stuck in place,
A metaphor for time and space.

It used to show a lovely view,
Of squirrels dancing in the dew.
Now all I see is dust and grime,
Oh what a funny waste of time!

My neighbors gave me odd looks too,
While I wrestled with the pane so blue.
Embracing the battle with all my might,
Just me and my window, what a sight!

If I could just turn back the clock,
To days when I'd unlock the lock.
Oh, where have those good times gone?
I wish this window just went on!

The Pathway of Reverie

In dreams I walk a path so bright,
With slippers on, oh what a sight!
But tripping on a stone or two,
I tumble, laugh, and then pursue.

Pastime tales in a sunlit park,
A chase with shadows, oh so stark.
Got lost with friends in laughter's embrace,
Only to find my shoes misplaced!

The echoes of youth, they cheer me on,
While squirrels giggle at every yawn.
In my mind, it's all a spree,
Except for those who still owe me a fee!

So let's retrace those joyful steps,
Where no one knows the place where we leapt.
In memory's glow, we'll twirl anew,
With tales of the silly things we blew!

Tides of Time and Reflection

The waves come in, then out they go,
With memories that ebb and flow.
I paddle out to catch old dreams,
Only to find they're bursting at the seams!

With a splash and a laugh on the shore,
Those tides of time, who could ask for more?
A bucket list that's filled with sand,
As shrimps conspire to shake my hand.

Mom once said, "Don't look too hard,
You might just find an old guitar."
Oh dear, it's out of tune and rusty,
But hey, it still feels kind of trusty!

So let the tides roll back again,
Where the seagulls swoop and the fish all grin.
In waves of quirks and laughter bent,
Each ripple sings of time well spent.

Lanterns in the Mist of Memory

In the mist, where lanterns glow,
I trip on thoughts both fast and slow.
Ghostly giggles fill the air,
As I search for a forgotten chair.

The shadows dance, oh such a show,
With mortal friends who don't quite know.
Their tales unfold in twinkling lights,
Of secret elves and silly fights.

I bump into a wall of haze,
It feels like I'm caught in a maze.
"Was that you in that silly hat?"
"Oh wait, I'm lost! Where am I at?"

Yet through the fog, I can still see,
The laughter from those who were once free.
So let's get lost every now and then,
In lanterns' glow, we'll laugh again!

Threads of the Unseen Past

In an attic high, with dust on the beams,
I found a hat that whispered my dreams.
It claimed to belong to an uncle named Lou,
Who danced in a chicken suit, who knew just what to do.

Old photos confide, with smiles like a grin,
A cousin with two heads and a thrift store win.
Their laughter still echoes, mocking my scheme,
As I try on their clothes, in search of a meme.

I tripped over relics, a shoe from a clown,
It squeaked as I stumbled and fell to the ground.
With each quirky item, a tale they narrate,
Life's a comical ride, don't let it wait.

So I'll gather these threads, each stitch bursts with fun,
Weaving tales from the past, and I'm never done.
With a wink to the specters that join me to laugh,
In this fashion of folly, I'm the photograph.

Reflections in the Glass

Peering at portraits hung high on the wall,
A pirate with parrots, what a sight to enthrall!
His eye patch is crooked, his smile's a bit sly,
He winks through the glass, oh my, oh my!

The mirror's a jester, it laughs back at me,
With weird faces and wigs, such a sight to see.
The reflections giggle, a band of the bold,
Each glance gets weirder, stories retold.

A royal in bloom, with a dress made of cheese,
Prances around, leaves me weak in the knees.
And right by her side, poodles in skirts,
Dancing a jig, rolling out all their quirks.

Tales trapped in the glass, nothing serious passed,
Moments of mirth, through the looking-glass cast.
So raise a toast to the whimsy and cheer,
For laughter's reflection keeps the past near!

The Pathway of What Was

There's a lane made of giggles, where shadows once fell,
Where socks go to vanish, they tell a wild tale.
Each step down this path, I bump into a cat,
Wearing sunglasses, and a bit of a hat.

He points to a fragment, an old rubber shoe,
Claiming it once danced on a stage made of stew.
I snicker and wonder, could it really be true?
A theater of veggies, a whimsical view!

Around every corner, odd creatures appear,
A duck in a tux, putting on quite the cheer.
He quacks out a tune, with a wink and a spin,
As confetti rained down, oh let the fun begin!

So I stroll down this pathway, with laughter in tow,
Each echoing moment steals the dullness to stow.
For what has once been is a blend, sweet and spry,
With the humorous past, I just can't deny!

Ghosts of Moments Gone By

In the hall of the quirky, where giggles reside,
The ghosts of my past wear a mustache with pride.
Each bump in the night brings a chuckle or two,
A pirouetting specter in a polka-dot shoe.

From a dog in a top hat who sways to the beat,
To a grandpa who's juggling, oh isn't he neat?
They dance with abandon, on floorboards that creak,
While humming old tunes with a silly mystique.

Through the laughter they share, lost moments refound,
A fiesta of foolishness, joy all around.
With each fleeting glimpse, I'm enchanted, I sway,
As they whisper sweet nonsense, come join in the play!

So I tiptoe through memory, collecting the glee,
With ghosts who remind me of what used to be.
Time turns into laughter, a jolly ruckus,
Amongst these silly phantoms, let's not make a fuss!

Lintels of Lost Legacies

In the closet, old shoes lie,
Dancing dreams on cobwebs high.
A tatted sweater, I must confess,
Looks like it's wearing a lot of stress.

Nostalgic tunes play on a loop,
As I step in, a clumsy stoop.
Grandpa's fishing rod, maybe a prank,
Caught a catfish, or that's what he swank.

Jars of pickles, still on the shelf,
Once a feast, now a ghost of self.
The recipe's lost, much to my dread,
Guess it's hot dogs and chips instead.

Photographs piled, what a sight!
Balding heads in a fashion fright.
Each smile a story, each wink a tale,
Like squirrels in tuxedos, they never fail.

Memories' Gentle Passage

In the attic, dust bunnies play,
They tell of an unwritten ballet.
A pogo stick, rusted and bent,
Takes me back to my childhood rent.

Comic books scattered, heroes in capes,
Saved the world from villainous shapes.
But now I daydream of epic snacks,
Wasting hours with nerdy hacks.

Old diaries filled with teenage woes,
Spelling errors and awkward prose.
"In love with a boy named Ted," I sigh,
He thought I was just a chicken pie.

But raiding the fridge was always prime,
Finding leftover pizza a crime.
Laughter echoes through layers of time,
Mom's holler still plays, oh how it rhymes!

Gates to Time's Tapestry

A key from the junk drawer in my hand,
Unlocks humor in a foreign land.
Socks that were lost, now found in pairs,
Whispers of mischief beyond compare.

Each trinket, a memory to tease,
Yarn balls rolling with awkward ease.
My hamster's grave, a playful prank,
Named him Houdini, now he's in the tank.

Old records crackle, playing it cool,
Dancing like it's some goofy school.
The '70s style, wide hip and wide grin,
What a sight, let's spin it again!

So here's to the quirky and silly delights,
To moments that twinkle like starry nights.
Laughing with shadows that come out to play,
The treasures of yore, keep gloom at bay.

Whispers from the Twilight

In twilight's embrace, a whoopee cushion sings,
Echoing laughter, oh the joy it brings!
Forgotten toys jingle like chimes,
As memories dance to the rhythm of rhymes.

An old bicycle, tires all flat,
Rides through nostalgia, imagine that!
Going up hills, all pedaled in vain,
But somehow we loved every ridiculous gain.

Ghosts in the garden, playing charades,
Barking like dogs in the shadowy glades.
A scarecrow with style, in fringe and fluff,
Laughing at folks looking puzzled and gruff.

In laughter's embrace, we rewind the reel,
Every memory, a delightful meal.
So raise your glass to the moments that last,
For humor's the treasure, spirits amassed!

Thresholds of Memory

In a skirt too tight, I slipped and fell,
A memory flashes, oh what a smell!
Grandma's cookies were too hard to chew,
Yet here I am laughing, how can this be true?

The wallpaper peels, it tickles my nose,
Uncle Joe dances, in his shoes with holes.
A family photo, oh what a surprise,
With mustaches and wigs, we all looked like fries!

We raced to the fridge, who'd steal the pie?
Only to find, it was the cat's sly eye.
The clock chimed twelve, we carried a tune,
While the dog sang along, quite out of tune!

Now I stride through this hall with my socks mismatched,

Giggling at memories I've happily scratched.
Each step a reminder of laughter and cheer,
Thresholds that shimmer, always drawing me near.

Echoes from an Open Gate

There's a swing that squeaks, it knows all my fears,
I pushed it too hard, then flew through the years.
My brother called, 'Duck!' as I took to the sky,
But all I could do was giggle and fly!

With a garden gnome that talks in my dreams,
He tells tales of lemonade stands and sweet creams.
Each mischief we plotted, each prank that we pulled,
Frogs in the mailbox, our laughter was fueled!

A door led to chaos, a room full of noise,
Where girls turned to princesses and boys were just toys.
We wielded our capes as we leapt through the air,
While the dog played the trumpet, with flair so rare!

Now echoes will tattle on memories spent,
Of lunchbox surprises and the laughter we lent.
Beyond this wide gate, I can see all that's bright,
With laughter as shadows that dance in the light.

Whispers of Yesterday

I tiptoe back to when my bike had a bell,
And we raced through the streets, who could ride well?
With ketchup on pizza, a fashion faux pas,
Yet we thought we were stars, the best there ever was!

Then there were summers with sunscreen galore,
Slathering on layers 'til we couldn't take more.
But the tan lines were real and oh, the bright burns!
While laughter erupted at our clueless turns!

The treehouse stood tall, with secret codes read,
With snacks in a safe, for our brave hearts to tread.
Imagination ruled, we soared through the skies,
While mom called us home, we'd plead with our eyes!

Now whispers of laughter float gently in air,
With echoes of mischief, our hearts had to share.
In a world full of memories both silly and grand,
The lightness of youth, like grains of soft sand.

Time's Glistening Portals

A portal so shiny, it sparkles and sings,
With pink polka dots and whimsical wings.
In socks of odd colors, I tiptoe right through,
To moments of magic, and mischief anew!

Old video games, where our thumbs would race fast,
Cheering and laughing, hoping we'd last.
But someone would trip, or the dog would just bark,
And there we would tangle, in giggles till dark!

I stumble on memories tucked away tight,
Like wearing a cape through a backyard twilight.
The stories unfold with each glance that I steal,
And laughter erupts, oh what joy it will reveal!

Now I dance with the echoes, they twirl and they spin,
In this shiny old world, where the fun can begin.
Through magic and whimsy, I glide ever near,
With glistening moments, forever held dear.

Shadows Beneath the Archway

In the corner, dust bunnies creep,
Dreams of a time when vacuuming was cheap.
Old shoes hang like ghosts on the wall,
Maybe the mice are having a ball!

Underneath the old wooden frame,
A cat thinks this space is its claim to fame.
What stories could chairs tell if they spoke?
Probably something about an old, spilled yolk!

Lurking behind with a grin so wide,
Cats plotting adventures they cannot hide.
Photos with faces, hair wild as the trees,
Wondering if dad really scored with that cheese.

In the shadows where old tales collide,
Where laughter and snickers from history abide.
Oh, how we giggle at vintage attire,
Next to the couch where the furnace is higher.

Relics of Forgotten Days

Look at that clock, it's ticking away,
When we never cared 'bout the time of day.
Old magazines whisper secrets of lore,
Like who wore what, and who danced on the floor!

The fridge has magnets, a colorful past,
Spelling out names, hoping friendships will last.
Toys in the corner, now gathering dust,
Can they come back? Well, it's a must!

Pants from a decade, now two sizes too small,
Who thought that fashion was shaped like a ball?
A disco ball spins, but only in dreams,
Shining on memories and wild, goofy schemes.

Forgotten guitars with strings made of rust,
Sing to the tunes of what used to be thrust.
Oh, how they play out the tales of the day,
As we sit back with ice cream and sway!

Through the Veil of Time

What's that smell? It can't be the cat!
Oh wait, it's grandma's old velvet hat.
Worn at some shindig, quite the affair,
Made heads turn and left everyone in despair!

Old records groan when played on the turn,
Each scratch a memory, a lesson to learn.
With every spin, the dance floor ignites,
As we stumble and swirl into hilarious nights.

An old typewriter sits with its keys dull,
But stories were written with all the soul.
Teasing the ink with a flick of the wrist,
Creating the magic we know can't be missed.

Bad jokes are penned in every old book,
As if they knew all the laughs they'd hook.
Every crinkle and wrinkle a giggle, a twine,
Reminding us life twirls through moments divine.

The Passageway of Remembrance

In the hallway, echoes of laughter persist,
Adventures recounted, why'd we ever resist?
Old slippers lie waiting for someone to roam,
Wandering back to our collective home.

Socks that don't match, a unique fashion choice,
Each telling of stories that shout and rejoice.
Grandpa, with stories of mischief and snacks,
Promises made—no running in packs!

A tapestry woven of threads oh so bright,
Hangin' on walls by the flickering light.
What misadventures dwell in those seams?
Maybe a secret or two in their dreams!

We race through the hallway, exploring like kids,
While dust motes dance, and the world gently skids.
With every footstep, we're never quite lost,
In this timeless tryst, we count not the cost.

Through the Dust of Ages

In a trunk of odd old shoes,
I found my great-great's ballyhoo.
There's a sock with holes galore,
And letters with love—oh, what a chore!

A mirror cracked, my grandma's style,
Reflects a laugh, a silly smile.
She danced in petticoats with glee,
Said, "Life's a wig; just let it be!"

Dust bunnies where memories hide,
A ghostly dance, a jolly ride.
I dust off tales of grand pursuits,
And giggle at the old-time boots.

Each laugh a breeze, each smile a spark,
Through relics bright, I stroll the dark.
With every find, a chuckle's cast,
In the quirks that laugh back from the past.

Chasing Phantoms of Memory

Old photos where we look so spry,
Wearing big hats, oh my, oh my!
The prom poses, such silly flair,
My dad's wig? It vanished in air!

The ice cream fights on summer days,
With sticky hands and splattered sprays.
We chased our laughter down the lane,
While mom just sighed, "Let them remain!"

Ghosts of giggles fill the hall,
Where echoes of our playtime call.
I chase those shadows, hear their cheer,
Attempting to relive yesteryear.

Yet present me gives future me a wink,
As time flies by—just take a drink!
I'll sprinkle joy in every crack,
And summon laughter, never lack.

The Whispering Entrance

Once I found a doorway small,
That whispered secrets, one and all.
It giggled when I peeked inside,
"Join in the fun!" it seemed to chide.

A hat that danced upon the shelf,
Said, "Why not wear me, be yourself?"
With shoes that pranced and socks that sang,
I twirled and flipped, oh, what a clang!

Charming trinkets, each with flair,
A smiling mug, a cozy chair.
They chuckle soft, their stories fold,
In memories bright, both warm and bold.

So through this portal, I just laugh,
I trade my fears for this silly craft.
With every step, a happier stance,
In this whimsical, wacky dance.

Fractured Reflections

In a puddle, I saw my past,
A soda pop and a silly cast.
My childhood self, with candy in hand,
Frolics around, life oh so grand!

The trampoline with its wild bounce,
Gave us air like we could pounce.
We flipped and flopped, no care at all,
Until we crashed, then heard the call.

A face that grinned through a cracked frame,
"Let's bake a cake!" it claimed with fame.
The flour fight erupted with glee,
I had icing in my hair, oh me!

With fractured mirrors showing delight,
Reflecting moments both sunny and bright.
I raise a toast to memory's art,
For laughter lives in each silly part.

Through the Mirage of Memory

In a house where dust bunnies play,
I found old socks from yesterday.
They dance and twirl in shoes askew,
Reminding me of things I knew.

A cat with glasses reads the news,
My cereal told me it's got to choose.
Time-traveling toast makes me laugh,
But where in the world is my other half?

Grandma's wig hangs like a crow,
I swear it whispers tales of woe.
That time I danced in my pajamas,
Oh, what fun, but now it's drama!

I sip my tea in a cracked cup,
Where memories wake and then mix up.
With a grin at the silly sight,
I trip on past, then take flight!

Silent Invitations

An old chair creaks, invites my sigh,
'Remember when?' it seems to cry.
With squeaky springs and faded cloth,
I sit, a time-traveler is what I'm worth.

Pictures smile with painted laughter,
Each frown is a joke chasing after.
The dog in a hat? What a crow,
With paws on keys, oh, don't you know?

Ink spills secrets on yellowed sheets,
I read in rhythm, to old beats.
In this patch of dust, I find a dance,
With every step, I take my chance.

The cake on the shelf begins to grin,
With frosting tales of where I've been.
A laugh erupts, it rolls like waves,
In silent moments, the past misbehaves!

Keeper of Yesterday's Secrets

My closet holds a time machine,
With outfits worse than I have seen.
A polka dot dress with shoulder pads,
I wear it now and make the dads!

The mirror winks, then waves hello,
It claims to know all there is to know.
I spot my hair with quirks galore,
It tells me stories, then begs for more.

Elvis records make my kitchen dance,
While peanut butter sings a romance.
The fridge hums tunes of ancient cheese,
A symphony that makes me sneeze!

In the yard, a gnome starts to sway,
I ask him what he did today.
He just chuckles, under his hat,
And I smile wide, imagining that!

Lanterns of Distant Days

In the attic, a lantern glows bright,
Whispering tales of silly delight.
A mismatched sock, a pirate's hat,
Turns my lost thoughts into a spat!

The clock tick-tocks, tickles my ear,
Pet rocks report the gossip here.
A skateboard monster zooms on by,
Laughing at dreams as they fly high.

Balloons from a party long gone,
Float by with tales of joy to spawn.
With each pop, new giggles to boot,
I chase after them, in pursuit!

I twirl under fibs woven tight,
Laughing at shadows that bounce with fright.
Celebrating the whims of my past,
As lanterns flicker, I dance at last!

Steps Don't Fade

Footprints dance on the stair,
Echoing laughter fills the air.
Back to the days of socks and slides,
Where everyone's spirit joyfully hides.

Creaky steps tell tales of delight,
Where mischief sneaks in with the night.
Remember the time we played hide and seek,
In a world where childhood is still unique.

Forgotten games in the attic reside,
Where dust bunnies and giggles collide.
Each squeaky floorboard whispers a jest,
A reminder that growing up's quite the quest.

Through the twists of time, we prance,
In our hearts, we still take a chance.
Replaying those moments, oh what a blast,
Life's funny that way, it never quite lasts.

The Archive of Heartstrings

In a scrapbook made of whimsy and cheer,
Old photos wink, as if they're near.
Doodles and scribbles dance on a page,
Revealing the tales of an innocent age.

Letters from crushes, all crumpled and worn,
Romantic blunders make giggles reborn.
Poetry written in terrible rhyme,
Captured forever as sweet moments in time.

Each turn of a page, a treasure unfolds,
Stories of friendships, both new and old.
Clippings of laughter, and sometimes a tear,
In-archives of heartstrings that bring us near.

Locked in a chest, the memories gleam,
Funniest details ignite like a dream.
We're all just kids with a tale to share,
In this wild adventure of love and flair.

The Passageway of Forgotten Souls

Passages lined with quirky ads,
Whispers of laughter, oh so mad.
Here lives the ghost of the lunchroom tease,
Beneath the heading, 'Best Day: please!'

Colors faded on old cafeteria walls,
Where secrets echo through narrow halls.
Trading snacks like deals of old,
With stories about who once was bold.

With every turn, a jester appears,
Bringing back both laughter and tears.
As we shuffle through the forgotten years,
Celebrating mishaps, our biggest fears.

In this space, we dance on a whim,
Betting on who'd win the prankster's hymn.
Tales of trickery, all in good fun,
The spirits of laughter under the sun.

Glistening Doors of Memory

Glistening doors that creak with a grin,
Behind them lie stories where we've all been.
Adventures we've had with shades of the past,
In hallways of humor, forever will last.

Each knob a ticket to laughter and cheer,
Unlocking the moments we hold so dear.
Hide and seek games that turned into quests,
In treasure hunts where friendship invests.

Colorful moments with pranks on a spree,
Like finding your shoes tied into a tree.
Silliness lingers, a ghost with a smile,
As laughter reminds us, it's all been worthwhile.

So let's open those doors and wander about,
With giggles and grins, there's no room for doubt.
In glistening memories, we thrive and play,
Living our lives in the most funny way.

Fragments of Long-Gone Dreams

I found some socks from '93,
A time when they had swag, you see.
They smelled of pizza and some old tea,
Oh, the laughs of youth, how wild and free!

There's a jacket from my disco days,
With sequins shining in a daze.
I wore it once, or was it twice?
Now it's a relic, not so nice!

Posters peeling on the wall,
Of bands long dead, I hear their call.
They jammed in my head, oh what a rush,
Now it's just dust in a silent hush!

A box of toys I thought I'd lost,
Marbles, dolls, quite the cost!
I didn't know the memories could last,
Long after the playtime's past!

Beyond the Frame of Now

I peeked through frames of photos past,
Where hair was big and fashion vast.
Those hairstyles though, quite a fright,
How did we think they were just right?

Old dance moves from the living room,
A twist and shout, a funky boom!
Now I just shuffle, hope to sneak,
I dance like I'm in a sitcom's peak!

Remember flip phones? Such a tech dream,
Now they're just relics in a meme stream.
I text with thumbs, miss the old clang,
Now it's just emojis, let the phone hang!

There's a charm in those days gone cold,
When life was funny and stories bold.
I'll laugh at my past in a joyful spree,
Life's wild ride, oh, can't you see?

Paths Worn by Time's Footfall

Once I wore my shoes with flair,
With sequins glittering everywhere.
Now they're scuffed and oddly bent,
I dread the thought of where they went!

My bike was fast, it flew like wind,
Now it's a rusted friend, rescind.
I crashed it once, or was it twice?
Memories of pain, that can't be nice!

Picnics made on grassy knolls,
With sandwiches and plastic bowls.
Ketchup stains were quite the sign,
Of good times gone, oh how they shine!

A treehouse built, my fortress grand,
Now just a plank, it couldn't stand.
But every squeak and every cheer,
Brings me back, oh take me near!

Doors of Distant Echoes

I stumbled on a squeaky door,
With memories packed from days of yore.
It groaned and creaked, quite the sound,
Like ghosts of laughter all around!

Through halls where mischief ruled the day,
I'd hide and seek, oh what a play!
Now the echoes laugh and tease,
At clumsy stunts and scraped knees!

Grandma's cookies, they once smelled sweet,
Now I bake, but fail to compete.
I've burned a dozen, oh what a sight,
Still giggle at desserts taking flight!

Yet every door, a tale to tell,
Of mishaps grand and trips that fell.
I'll dance through life with joy and grace,
With echoes of laughter in this space!

www.ingramcontent.com/pod-product-compliance
Lightning Source LLC
Chambersburg PA
CBHW062113280426
43661CB00086B/567